KRISTEN'S VICTORY

ISBN - 979-8-9877804-0-4
Author Roberta Theriault
Illustrator Dom Sahadewa
Printed in the United States of America
First Printing Edition
For more information contact the author at robterrio27@yahoo.com

"To the memory of my parents, whose support, encouragement and guidance never let me down."

Nickeli's tail banged against the back seat as Kristen got into the truck.
He gave her a big sloppy doggy kiss on the face,

"SLURP!"
Kristen pushed Nickeli back.

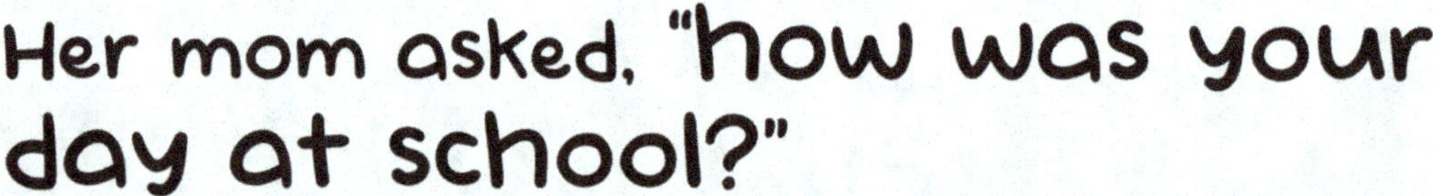

Her mom asked, "how was your day at school?"

"I'm definitely the dumbest kid in my class," Kristen said with tears in her eyes.

"I got 5 wrong on the spelling test and it's all because I'm deaf."
Her mom leaned over and hugged her tightly.

"Well, I think you're very smart," she told her.

"Think about all the things you do on the ranch. That takes a lot of Know how."
Kristen just nodded her head.

The next day was Saturday.
Kristen and Nickeli came out of the house, with Kristen, still wearing a frown.
She knew there was work to be done though and she reluctantly got started.

"Let's feed those hungry chickens," Kristen told Nickeli in sign language.

Nickeli was a friend and helper to Kristen, and he even knew some sign language. He was also very good at letting her know when someone was trying to get her attention, like her mom or dad.

Kristen eventually signed, "well at least I feed chickens really well." Nickeli barked and nudged one of the chickens with his nose. The chicken pecked Nickeli's nose back.

Kristen giggled. "Sometimes you make me laugh," she told him. "But I'm still sad."
Nickeli trotted over to Kristen and gave her a big sloppy doggy kiss on the face, "SLURP!"
"Thanks, Nickeli," she signed, "your kisses do help.... a little."

"Squirt, squirt. Squirt, squirt," went the goat's milk into the metal pail.

"I love milking these mama goats," Kristen told Nickeli. "I remember when I didn't know how. I had to practice a lot".

Just then a little smile shone on Kristen's face as she thought about learning to milk.

When Nickeli saw Kristen's smile, he scampered over and gave Kristen a big sloppy doggy kiss on the face, "SLURP!"
"Oh Nickeli, you're just plain silly," Kristen signed.

In the afternoon, Kristen asked her mom if she could go for a horseback ride with her friend Lisa. Lisa's parents were deaf too, but Lisa was not.

"I think a ride will help me feel better," Kristen told her mom. So, they saddled up and off they went with Nickeli close behind.

"Should we ride to the river?" Lisa asked Kristen.

"OK". Kristen signed back.

So, the horses clipped and clopped through the pasture, up the grassy hill, over the rocky slope and then down to the river. Kristen and Lisa were just about to cross the river when suddenly, Lisa's horse slipped on a wet rock and fell forward.

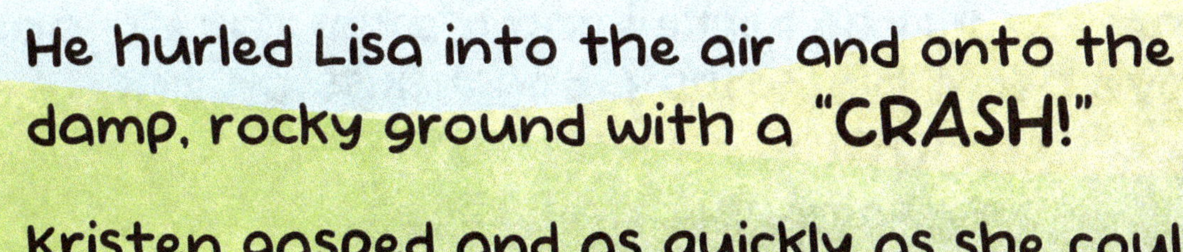

He hurled Lisa into the air and onto the damp, rocky ground with a "**CRASH!**"

Kristen gasped and as quickly as she could, jumped off her horse and ran right over to Lisa.

Lisa was crying and holding her leg. "It hurts really bad," she finally told Kristen. "I'll help you, don't worry," Kristen signed.

Kristen's eyes were wide open, and her hands were shaking. She didn't know what to do. Then suddenly, Nickeli came over to Lisa and gave her a big, sloppy, doggy kiss on the face, "SLURP!"

That gave Kristen an idea. "I'll send Nickeli for help," she told Lisa. "I'll tie my bandana to his collar and Mom and Dad will surely know that someone needs help."

And that's just what she did. She told Nickeli,
"Help! Go get Mom Nickeli! Help!"
Nickeli was off in a flash. He zoomed all the
way back to the ranch.

A little while later, Nickeli was back, and Kristen's mom and dad were with him.
"Good work!"

Kristen signed to Nickeli. Her mom and dad went over to check on Lisa.
"Lisa will be fine," her mom finally told Kristen.
"We'll get her right home."

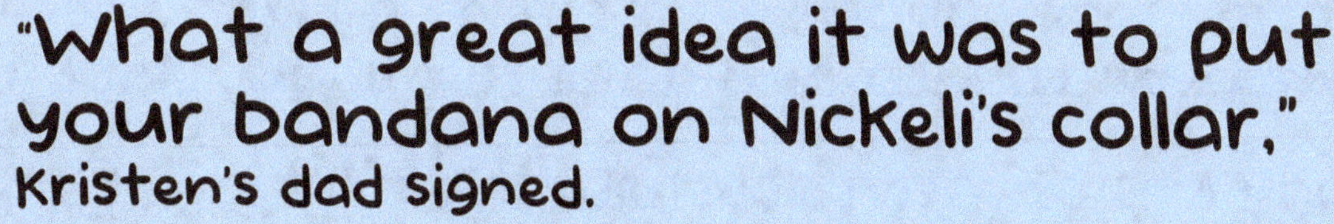

"What a great idea it was to put your bandana on Nickeli's collar," Kristen's dad signed.

"We might never have known you were in trouble." Kristen smiled ear to ear with pride.

"Maybe I'm pretty smart after all," she thought.

As they were about to leave the river, Nickeli went over to Lisa and gave her a big, sloppy, doggy kiss on her face, "SLURP!"

Kristen smiled and gave Nickeli a kiss on his head and a big hug and they walked back to the ranch together.